HEALTHY COOKING

LOW
SALT

TIGER BOOKS INTERNATIONAL
LONDON

FOR A FITTER BODY

2437
This edition published 1993 by Tiger Books International PLC, London
© 1991 Coombe Books
ISBN 1-85501-312-6

Introduction

The mineral sodium chloride, or salt, has been used over the centuries for its medicinal properties as well as its flavouring and preserving qualities. Why then should we want a low salt diet? To answer this we must look more closely at the need for and the use of salt by our bodies.

Salt is essential to the balance of acids in the blood and the maintenance of the fluid content of our cells. Without a certain amount of salt we would suffer from severe muscular cramps and bodily degeneration. The quantity that our bodies require, however, is actually very small and is easily obtainable from the whole, fresh foods we eat daily without the need to add more.

The correct balance of salt in the body is maintained by the kidneys, which remove excess salt. Too great a salt intake can lead to fluid retention, places a strain on the kidneys and can even lead to problems such as depression.

More commonly, though, high sodium levels in the body can be directly linked to abnormally high blood pressure, or hypertension. All Western countries with a high salt consumption have a problem with high blood pressure. This, along with obesity and smoking, has been found to be one of the major causes of fatal heart disease.

Unfortunately, the taste for salt is addictive and people tend to feel that their bodies require large amounts. Whilst this may be true in a few instances, under normal conditions this is simply not the case. People simply become accustomed to the excessive use of salt and feel that without it their food lacks taste. Gradually their bodies remove less of the excess sodium and problems begin.

In this book, the recipes rely on alternative flavourings to enhance the taste of food. These ingredients may not have been available in ancient times when the taste for salt was established, but they are now easy to obtain. The recipes are simple to prepare and show just how easily you can adapt to a pattern of eating that will, with time, reduce your need for the flavour of salt.

MAKES 24

CHEESY AVOCADO SAVOURIES

A delightful combination of avocado, nuts and cheese, this recipe doesn't need the addition of salt to enhance the taste of these delicious party savouries.

1 ripe avocado
30ml/2 tbsps single cream or natural yogurt
1 clove garlic, crushed
5ml/1 tsp lemon juice
90g/3oz finely grated Cheddar cheese
5ml/1 tsp ready-made English mustard
30g/1oz fresh white breadcrumbs
3 spring onions, finely chopped
Freshly ground black pepper, to taste
30ml/2 tbsps freshly chopped parsley
60g/2oz toasted, chopped almonds

Step 5 Form teaspoonfuls of the avocado mixture into small balls using your hands.

Step 7 Roll each ball into the finely chopped parsley, coating them thoroughly.

Step 1 After cutting, carefully twist the avocado apart to make two halves.

1. Cut the avocado in half lengthways and carefully twist it apart.

2. Remove the stone afd peel away the skin from the avocado halves using a sharp knife.

3. Mash the avocado flesh into a medium-sized bowl using a fork or a small potato masher.

4. Stir the cream or yogurt, garlic, lemon juice, grated cheese, mustard, breadcrumbs, onions and pepper into the mashed avocado. Mix together well with a fork until a stiff paste results.

5. Using your hands, roll teaspoonfuls of the avocado mixture into small balls.

6. Spread the parsley onto one small plate and the almonds onto another.

7. Roll half the number of avocado balls into the finely chopped parsley pressing it gently into the surface to coat thoroughly.

8. Roll the remaining avocado balls into the almonds in the same manner.

9. Refrigerate the coated snacks for 40 minutes before serving with drinks.

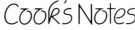

Cook's Notes

 Time
Preparation takes 30 minutes, plus 30 minutes refrigeration time.

 Preparation
It is most important to keep the mixture cool when preparing these snacks. If you have difficulty forming the mixture into small balls, refrigerate for at least 30 minutes.

 Variation
Use finely chopped walnuts instead of the almonds, and Stilton cheese instead of the Cheddar.

MAKES 36

STUFFED EGGS

Stuffed eggs make an attractive, and deliciously different, party appetiser.

18 small eggs, or quail eggs
60g/2oz unsalted butter
1 clove garlic, crushed
90g/3oz cooked, peeled prawns, finely chopped
2.5ml/½ tsp finely chopped fresh basil
Freshly ground black pepper, to taste

1. Cook the eggs in boiling water for 5 minutes. Drain, and plunge them immediately into cold water.

2. Allow the eggs to cool completely, then remove the shells. Rinse and drain.

3. Cut each egg in half lengthways and carefully remove the yolks.

4. Put the yolks into a large bowl and beat in the butter and garlic. Mix well.

5. Add the prawns, basil and pepper to the creamed egg yolk mixture. Beat thoroughly until a soft consistency results.

6. Fill each egg white half with a little of the prepared mixture, piling it attractively into the cavity left by the egg yolk.

7. Refrigerate until required.

Step 4 Cream the butter and garlic into the egg yolks, beating thoroughly to mix well.

Step 6 Pile equal amounts of the filling mixture into the halved egg whites, forking it attractively to serve.

Step 3 Using a sharp knife, halve the hard-boiled eggs lengthways.

Cook's Notes

Time
Preparation takes 15 minutes, cooking takes 5 minutes.

Variation
Use flaked white crab meat instead of the prawns. For a more exotic dish, use quails eggs instead of hens' eggs.

Serving Idea
Serve the filled egg halves on a plate which has been garnished with frisee lettuce leaves, and tiny pieces of red pepper.

MAKES 350g/12oz

SPICED NUTS

Everyone likes to nibble nuts with drinks at a party, but most contain very high quantities of salt. These delicious spiced nuts contain no salt, are extremely easy to make, and can be prepared well in advance.

30ml/2 tbsps corn or vegetable oil
120g/4oz fresh peanuts, shelled and husked
120g/4oz blanched almonds
120g/4oz fresh cashew nuts, shelled and husked
2.5ml/½ tsp ground ginger
2.5ml/½ tsp ground cinnamon
2.5ml/½ tsp cayenne pepper

1. Heat the oil in a large frying pan.

Step 2 Stir the nuts into the hot oil, making sure they are evenly coated.

Step 3 Sprinkle the spices over the nuts and mix well.

Step 4 Spread the nuts in an even layer on an ovenproof baking dish.

2. Stir in the nuts, mixing well to coat evenly with the hot oil.

3. Sprinkle the spices over the nuts and stir well to coat evenly.

4. Transfer the nuts to an ovenproof dish, spreading them in an even layer.

5. Toast the nuts for 10-15 minutes in a preheated oven, 190°C/375°F/Gas Mark 5.

6. To prevent the nuts from burning, turn them with a fish slice or palette knife once or twice during the cooking time.

Cook's Notes

Time
Preparation takes 10 minutes, cooking takes 10-15 minutes.

Cook's Tip
Prepare these nuts in advance and store them for up to 2 weeks in an airtight container.

Variation
Use hazelnuts instead of cashew nuts, and ground cardamom, cumin and chilli powder instead of the ginger, cinnamon and cayenne pepper.

SERVES 4-6

SPICY CHILLI BEAN SOUP

This 'complete meal' soup certainly doesn't need salt to bring out the full flavour of the ingredients.

90ml/3 tbsps vegetable oil
2 onions, roughly chopped
1 clove garlic, crushed
15ml/1 tbsp ground cumin
10ml/2 tsps ground paprika
1 red or green chilli pepper, seeded and finely chopped
225g/8oz minced beef
790g/1¾lbs canned tomatoes, chopped
860ml/1½ pints chicken or vegetable stock
90g/3oz tomato purée
5ml/1 tsp oregano
1 bay leaf
140ml/¼ pint beer
Freshly ground black pepper
120g/4oz each of canned red kidney beans, chick peas, and white pinto beans, drained and thoroughly rinsed.

1. Heat the oil in a large, heavy-based saucepan.

2. Add the onion and garlic and cook slowly until they become transparent.

3. Stir in the cumin, paprika and chilli pepper. Increase the heat and cook quickly for 30 seconds, stirring all the time.

4. Add the meat and cook until lightly browned, breaking up any large pieces with a fork.

5. Add the tomatoes and their juice, the stock, tomato purée, oregano, bay leaf, beer and ground pepper. Stir well, then bring to the boil.

6. Cover and simmer for approximately 50 minutes, checking the level of liquid several times during the cooking and adding more water if the soup seems too dry.

7. During the last 15 minutes of cooking, add the drained beans, stirring them in to mix well.

Step 4 Add the meat and cook until lightly browned, breaking up any large pieces with a fork.

Step 7 Add the drained beans to the soup during the last 15 minutes of cooking time.

Cook's Notes

Time
Preparation takes 30 minutes, cooking takes 1 hour.

Freezing
This soup freezes well.

Cook's Tip
If you cannot buy canned beans and chick peas, use 60g/2oz each of dried beans. Soak them overnight and cook thoroughly for 1 hour before using in this recipe.

Serving Idea
Serve with a mixed garnish of chopped fresh tomatoes, chopped spring onions and cubed avocado which has been sprinkled with lemon juice.

SERVES 4-6

COURGETTE SOUP WITH LEMON

The fresh taste of lemon and courgettes makes a delicious soup which can be served either hot or cold.

1 medium-sized onion, thinly sliced
30ml/2 tbsps olive oil
450g/1lb courgettes, topped, tailed and sliced
Finely grated rind and juice of 1 large lemon
450ml/¾ pint chicken stock
Freshly ground black pepper
2 egg yolks
200ml/⅓ pint natural yogurt

1. In a large pan, fry the onion gently in the olive oil for 3 minutes until it is just transparent.

2. Add the courgettes and fry for a further 2-3 minutes.

Step 1 In a large pan gently fry the onion until it is just transparent.

3. Stir in all remaining ingredients except the egg yolks and yogurt, cover and simmer for 20 minutes.

4. Transfer the soup to a liquidiser or food processor, and blend until smooth.

Step 4 Blend the soup in a liquidiser, or food processor, until it is smooth.

Step 5 Mix together the egg yolks and yogurt in a small jug or bowl.

5. Mix the egg yolks into the yogurt and stir into the blended soup.

6. Reheat the soup gently, stirring all the time until it thickens.

7. Serve hot at this stage, or transfer to a refrigerator and chill thoroughly.

Cook's Notes

Time
Preparation takes 20 minutes, plus chilling time, cooking takes 25 minutes.

Serving Idea
Serve the soup with a garnish of thinly sliced courgettes and light French toasts.

Preparation
Great care must be taken not to boil the soup once the egg yolks have been added, otherwise the mixture will curdle.

Freezing
This soup can be frozen, but not after the egg yolks have been added. Freeze before this stage, defrost and then finish the recipe as described.

SERVES 4

SEVICHE

In this traditional Mexican dish the raw fish is 'cooked' in a mixture of oil and lime juice. Quick and easy to prepare, seviche makes a highly nutritious and very tasty appetizer.

450g/1lb fresh cod fillet
Juice and grated rind of 2 limes
1 small shallot, finely chopped
1 green chilli pepper, seeded and finely chopped
5ml/1 tsp ground coriander
1 small green pepper, seeded and sliced
1 small red pepper, seeded and sliced
15ml/1 tbsp freshly chopped parsley
15ml/1 tbsp freshly chopped coriander
4 spring onions, finely chopped
30ml/2 tbsps olive oil
Freshly ground black pepper
1 small lettuce, to serve

1. Carefully remove the skin from the cod fillets.

2. Using a sharp knife cut the fish into very thin strips across the grain.

3. Put the fish strips into a large bowl and pour over the lime juice.

4. Stir in the grated lime rind, shallot, chilli pepper and ground coriander. Mix well.

5. Cover the bowl with plastic wrap or a damp cloth and refrigerate for 24 hours, stirring occasionally during this

time to ensure that the fish remains well coated in the lime.

6. Mix the sliced peppers, spring onions and the fresh herbs together in a large bowl.

7. Put the fish mixture into a colander and drain off the juice.

8. Put the drained fish into the pepper mixture and stir in the oil, mixing well to coat evenly. Add freshly ground pepper to taste.

9. Finely shred the lettuce and arrange on a serving plate.

10. Spread the fish mixture attractively over the lettuce and serve immediately, garnished with slices of lime, if liked.

Step 2 Cut the cod fillet across the grain into very thin slices.

Step 1 Using a sharp knife, carefully remove the skin from the cod fillets.

Step 5 After refrigerating for 24 hours, the fish should have a cooked appearance.

Cook's Notes

Time
Preparation takes 20 minutes, plus 24 hours standing time.

Variation
Use hake or salmon in place of the cod in this recipe.

Serving Idea
As well as being an interesting appetizer, Seviche can also be served with pitta breads for a tasty lunch.

SERVES 6-8

TERRINE OF SPINACH AND CHICKEN

This superb terrine is ideal when you want to impress your guests with a delicious appetizer.

225g/8oz chicken breasts, boned and skinned
2 egg whites
120g/4oz fresh white breadcrumbs
450g/1lb fresh spinach, washed
15ml/1 tbsp each of fresh finely chopped chervil, chives and tarragon
Freshly ground black pepper
280ml/½ pint double cream
60g/2oz finely chopped walnuts
Pinch nutmeg

Step 4 The spinach should be cooked until it is just wilted, using only the water that clings to the leaves and adding no extra liquid.

1. Cut the chicken into small pieces.

2. Put the cut chicken, 1 egg white and half of the breadcrumbs into a food processor. Blend until well mixed.

3. Put the spinach into a large saucepan and cover with a tight-fitting lid.

4. Cook the spinach for 3 minutes, or until it has just wilted.

5. Remove the chicken mixture from the food processor and rinse the bowl.

6. Put the spinach into the food processor along with the herbs, the remaining egg white and breadcrumbs. Blend until smooth.

7. Season the chicken mixture with a little pepper and add half of the cream. Mix well to blend thoroughly.

8. Add the remaining cream to the spinach along with the walnuts and the nutmeg. Beat this mixture well to blend thoroughly.

9. Line a 450g/1lb loaf tin with greaseproof paper. Lightly oil this with a little vegetable oil.

10. Pour the chicken mixture into the base of the tin and spread evenly.

11. Carefully pour the spinach mixture over the chicken mixture, and smooth the top with a palette knife.

12. Cover the tin with lightly oiled aluminium foil and seal this tightly around the edges.

13. Stand the tin in a roasting dish and pour enough warm water into the dish to come halfway up the sides of the tin.

14. Cook the terrine in a preheated oven 160°C/325°F/ Gas Mark 3 for 1 hour, or until it is firm.

15. Put the terrine into the refrigerator and chill for at least 12 hours.

16. Carefully lift the terrine out of the tin and peel off the paper. To serve, cut the terrine into thin slices with a sharp knife.

Cook's Notes

 Time
Preparation takes 25 minutes, cooking takes 1 hour.

 Serving Idea
Serve slices of the terrine on individual serving plates garnished with a little salad.

 Watchpoint
Do not overcook the terrine or attempt to cook it any more quickly than the recipe states, otherwise it will curdle and spoil.

SERVES 4

ANDALUCIAN AUBERGINES

This delicious aubergine dish is highly reminiscent of Andalucia in Spain where tomatoes, rice and tuna fish are very popular ingredients.

4 small aubergines
45ml/3 tbsps olive oil
1 small onion, finely chopped
1 clove garlic, crushed
120g/4oz cooked whole grain rice
200g/7oz can tuna in oil, drained and fish coarsely flaked
15ml/1 tbsp mayonnaise
5ml/1 tsp curry powder
4 fresh tomatoes, skinned, seeded and chopped
15ml/1 tbsp coarsely chopped parsley
Freshly ground black pepper

1. Cut the aubergines in half lengthways. Score the cut surfaces lightly with a sharp knife at regular intervals.

2. Brush the scored surface lightly with 1 tbsp of the olive oil and place the aubergines on a greased baking sheet.

3. Bake the aubergines in a preheated oven 190°C/375°F/Gas Mark 5, for 15 minutes, or until beginning to soften.

4. Cool the aubergines slightly, then carefully scoop the centre flesh from each half. Take care that you do not break the skin at this stage.

5. Fry the chopped onion gently in the remaining 30 ml/2 tbsps of olive oil for 3 minutes, or until they are just transparent.

6. Add the garlic and the aubergine flesh, and fry for a further 2 minutes. Season to taste with pepper.

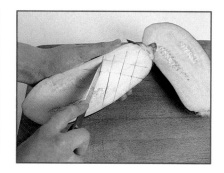

Step 1 Taking care not to break the skins, score the cut surface of the aubergine halves at regular intervals with a sharp, pointed knife.

Step 4 Carefully scoop the baked aubergine flesh out of each half, keeping the skin shells intact.

7. Add the rice, flaked tuna, mayonnaise, curry powder, tomatoes, parsley and black pepper to the aubergine mixture, and mix together well.

8. Pile equal amounts of this rice and tuna filling into the aubergine shells. Return the filled aubergines to the ovenproof baking dish. Brush with the remaining olive oil, and bake in the oven for a further 25 minutes. Serve piping hot.

Cook's Notes

Time
Preparation will take 40 minutes, cooking takes about 50 minutes.

Serving Idea
Serve with a crisp mixed leaf salad and black olives.

Preparation
Use a serrated grapefruit knife to remove the baked aubergine flesh without tearing the skins.

Variation
For a tasty vegetarian variation, use 175g/6oz button mushrooms in place of the tuna.

MAKES 1

HAM AND GREEN PEPPER OMELETTE

Use 'tendersweet' ham in this recipe to keep the salt content as low as possible.

3 eggs
30ml/2 tbsps milk
Freshly ground black pepper
15ml/1 tbsp vegetable oil
30g/1oz chopped green pepper
2 tomatoes, peeled, seeded and roughly chopped
60g/2oz lean ham, cut into small dice

1. Break the eggs into the bowl and beat in the milk and pepper.

2. Heat the oil in a omelette pan and fry the green pepper until it is just soft.

3. Stir in the tomatoes and the ham. Heat through for 1 minute.

4. Pour the egg mixture into the frying pan over the vegetables. Stir the mixture briskly with a wooden spoon, until it begins to cook.

5. As the egg begins to set, lift it slightly and tilt the pan to allow the uncooked egg underneath.

6. When the egg on top is still slightly creamy, fold the omelette in half and slip it onto a serving plate. Serve immediately

Step 5 Lift the cooked egg with a fork and tilt the frying pan to allow uncooked egg underneath.

Step 6 Fold the omelette in half whilst the top of the egg is still slightly creamy.

Step 2 Gently fry the pepper in hot oil until it begins to soften.

Cook's Notes

Time
Preparation takes about 15 minutes, cooking takes 5 minutes.

Serving Idea
Serve the omelette with a crisp leaf salad and French bread.

Cook's Tip
To peel tomatoes easily, cut a small cross into the skin and drop them into boiling water for about 10 seconds, then plunge into cold water. This loosens the peel.

Variation
Use any selection of your favourite vegetables to vary this delicious dish.

SERVES 4

TOMATOES PROVENÇALE

Use fragrant herbs from the Provence region of France to complement sweet tomatoes, and no salt will be required to enhance their flavour.

4 large ripe tomatoes
30ml/2 tbsps olive oil
1 clove garlic, crushed
2x1.25cm/½-inch-thick slices white bread, crusts removed
15ml/1 tbsp chopped parsley
10ml/2 tsps chopped thyme or marjoram
Freshly ground black pepper

Step 1 Using a grapefruit knife, carefully scoop the flesh out of each tomato half, making sure that you do not break the shells.

1. Cut the tomatoes in half and carefully cut out the tomato pulp using a grapefruit knife.

2. Put the tomato pulp into a sieve and press out the juice using the back of a wooden spoon. Put the dry tomato pulp into a large bowl.

3. Mix the olive oil and garlic together. Brush both sides of the bread with this mixture and leave to stand for 10 minutes.

4. Using a sharp knife, chop the oiled bread and the herbs together until they are well mixed and fine textured.

Stir this into the tomato pulp and add black pepper.

5. Press the tomato filling into the tomato shells, piling it slightly above the cut edge.

Step 2 Put the tomato pulp into a sieve and press out as much juice as possible using the back of a wooden spoon.

Step 4 Using a sharp knife, chop the herbs and the oiled bread together until they are as fine as breadcrumbs.

6. Arrange the tomatoes on an ovenproof dish and grill under a low heat for 5 minutes.

7. Raise the temperature of the grill to high and brown the tomatoes on top for a few seconds. Serve at once.

Cook's Notes

Time
Preparation takes 15-20 minutes. Cooking time takes 5 minutes.

Cook's Tip
Prepare the tomatoes in advance and grill them just before serving.

Serving Idea
Serve with a rice salad for a light lunch.

SERVES 4-6

MUSHROOM SALAD

Mushrooms have a flavour all of their own and do not require salt.
This salad can be made using cultivated
mushrooms, but it is extra special when prepared with wild ones.

450g/1lb button or oyster mushrooms
1 medium-sized onion
45ml/3 tbsps vegetable oil
15ml/1 tbsp freshly chopped parsley
1 cucumber, finely diced
3-4 tomatoes, peeled, seeded and sliced
60ml/4 tbsps olive oil
15ml/1 tbsp white wine vinegar
Freshly ground black pepper
1 small iceberg lettuce

1. Trim the mushrooms and rub clean with a damp cloth.

2. Slice the mushrooms very thinly and chop the onions finely.

Step 2 Slice the mushrooms very thinly with a sharp knife.

3. Heat the vegetable oil in a large frying pan and gently sauté the mushrooms and onions for 2-3 minutes, or until they are just soft. Allow to cool.

Step 3 Fry the mushrooms and onions gently in hot oil until they just begin to soften.

Step 4 Add the parsley, cucumber and tomatoes to the mushrooms, mixing well to combine ingredients evenly.

4. When the mushrooms have cooled, stir in the parsley, cucumber and tomatoes.

5. Mix together the oil, vinegar and pepper in a small jug, and pour over all the other ingredients.

6. Stir gently to coat evenly, and refrigerate for 1-2 hours.

7. Shred the lettuce finely and arrange on a serving plate. Spread the chilled mushrooms evenly over the lettuce.

Cook's Notes

Time
Preparation takes 10 minutes, cooking takes 5 minutes. Chilling time is a minimum of 2 hours.

Cook's Tip
The salad can be prepared a day in advance and stored in the refrigerator until required.

Serving Ideas
Serve with Melba toast or crusty wholemeal rolls.

SERVES 4

SZECHWAN MEATBALLS

Szechwan is a region of China that lends its name to a style of cookery which includes many spices, most notably ginger. The spicy nature of these dishes means they require no salt.

90g/3oz blanched almonds
450g/1lb minced beef
5ml/1 tsp grated fresh ginger
1 clove garlic, crushed
½ large green pepper, seeded and chopped
Dash of Szechwan, chilli, or Tabasco sauce
30ml/2 tbsps soy sauce
Oil for frying
45ml/3 tbsps soy sauce
120ml/4 fl oz vegetable stock
15ml/1 tbsp rice wine or white wine vinegar
10ml/2 tsps honey
15ml/1 tbsp sherry
15ml/1 tbsp cornflour
4 spring onions, sliced diagonally

blended.

4. Divide the mixture into16 and roll each piece into small meatballs on a lightly floured board.

5. Heat a little oil in a large frying pan and lay in about half of the meatballs in a single layer.

6. Cook the meatballs over a low heat for about 20 minutes, turning them frequently until they are well browned all over.

7. Transfer to a serving dish and keep warm while you cook the remaining meatballs. Set aside as before.

8. Stir the 3 tbsps soy sauce, stock and vinegar into the frying pan and bring to the boil. Boil briskly for about 30 seconds.

Step 1 Toast the almonds under a low grill until pale gold in colour, stirring them frequently to prevent them from burning.

Step 6 Gently fry the meatballs in the hot oil until they are evenly browned.

1. Spread the almonds evenly onto a grill pan, and grill under a low heat for 3-4 minutes, or until lightly toasted. Stir the almonds often to prevent them from burning.

2. Chop the almonds coarsely using a large sharp knife.

3. In a large bowl, combine the chopped almonds with the meat, ginger, garlic, green pepper, Szechwan sauce, and the 2 tbsps of soy sauce. Use a wooden spoon, or your hands, to ensure that the ingredients are well

9. Add the honey and stir until dissolved.

10. Blend the sherry and cornflour together in a small bowl, and add this into the hot sauce. Cook, stirring all the time, until thickened.

11. Arrange the meatballs on a serving dish and sprinkle with the sliced spring onions. Pour the sauce over, and serve.

Cook's Notes

Time
Preparation takes about 20 minutes, cooking takes 40 minutes.

Serving Idea
Serve with boiled rice and a tomato salad.

Freezing
The meatballs will freeze uncooked for up to 3 months. The sauce should be prepared freshly when required.

SERVES 4-6

CHICKEN CACCIATORE

*The use of herbs, wine and vinegar in this delicious Italian family meal gives a
wonderful, hearty flavour without the need for salt.*

60ml/4 tbsps olive oil
1.5kg/3lbs chicken pieces
2 onions, sliced
3 cloves garlic, crushed
225g/8oz button mushrooms, quartered
140ml/¼ pint red wine
15ml/1 tbsp wine vinegar
15ml/1 tbsp fresh chopped parsley
10ml/2 tsps fresh chopped oregano
10ml/2 tsps fresh chopped basil
1 bay leaf
450g/1lb tinned tomatoes
140ml/¼ pint chicken stock
Freshly ground black pepper
Pinch of sugar

1. In a large frying pan heat the oil and lay the chicken pieces, skin side down, in one layer.

2. Brown for 3-4 minutes, then turn each piece over.

Continue turning the chicken portions until all surfaces are well browned.

3. Remove the chicken portions to a plate and keep warm.

4. Add the onions and garlic to the oil and chicken juices in the frying pan. Cook lightly for 2-3 minutes, or until they are just beginning to brown.

5. Add the mushrooms to the pan and cook for about 1 minute, stirring constantly.

6. Pour the wine and vinegar into the pan and boil rapidly to reduce to about half the original quantity.

7. Add the herbs, bay leaf and tomatoes, stirring well to break up the tomatoes.

8. Stir in the chicken stock and season with pepper and sugar.

9. Return the chicken to the tomato sauce and cover with a tight fitting lid. Simmer for about 1 hour, or until the chicken is tender.

Step 2 Turn the chicken frequently until all the outer surfaces are golden brown.

Step 7 Break the tomatoes in the pan by pressing them gently with the back of a wooden spoon.

Cook's Notes

Time
Preparation takes about 20 minutes, cooking takes 1 hour 15 minutes.

Serving Idea
Serve with rice or pasta, and a mixed salad.

Variation
Use the delicious sauce in this recipe with any other meat of your choice.

Freezing
This dish freezes well for up to 3 months. Defrost thoroughly and reheat by simmering for at least 30 minutes before serving.

SERVES 4

SWEDISH HERRINGS

The Swedes adore the flavour of fresh dill and mild mustard.
This combination is all that is required
to bring out the full flavour of fresh herring.

60ml/4 tbsps fresh chopped dill
90ml/3 fl oz mild Swedish mustard
30ml/2 tbsps lemon juice or white wine
4-8 fresh herrings, cleaned, but heads and tails left on
30ml/2 tbsps unsalted butter, melted
Freshly ground black pepper
Lemon wedges and whole sprigs of fresh dill, to garnish

Step 2 Using a very sharp knife, cut 3 shallow slits just through the skin on each side of the fish.

Step 1 Mix the dill, mustard and lemon juice or white wine together in a small bowl, mixing well to blend all these ingredients thoroughly.

Step 3 Spread the mustard mixture over each fish, carefully pushing a little into each cut.

1. Put the dill, mustard and lemon juice or white wine into a small bowl and mix together thoroughly.

2. Using a sharp knife, cut three shallow slits through the skin on both sides of each fish.

3. Spread half of the mustard mixture over one side of each fish, pushing some of the mixture into each cut.

4. Drizzle a little of the melted butter over the fish and grill under a preheated hot grill for 5-6 minutes.

5. Using a fish slice, carefully turn each fish over, and spread with the remaining dill and mustard mixture.

6. Drizzle over the remaining butter and grill for a further 5-6 minutes, or until the fish is thoroughly cooked.

7. Sprinkle the fish with black pepper and serve garnished with the dill sprigs and lemon wedges.

Cook's Notes

Time
Preparation takes 10 minutes, cooking takes 12-15 minutes.

Cook's Tip
To be sure that the fish you are buying are completely fresh, make sure that the skins are moist and the eyes are bright.

Variation
Use mackerel instead of the herrings in this recipe.

Serving Idea
Serve with new potatoes and green vegetables.

SERVES 4

SWEET AND SOUR TURKEY MEATBALLS

These easy-to-prepare turkey meatballs are served with a highly flavoured sweet and sour sauce.

1 small onion, finely chopped
30ml/2 tbsps olive oil
450g/1lb raw turkey
1 clove garlic, peeled and crushed
30ml/2 tbsps fresh parsley, chopped
30ml/2 tbsps blanched almonds, finely chopped
Freshly ground black pepper
1.25ml/¼ tsp mixed spice
15ml/1 tbsp chopped raisins
30ml/2 tbsps fresh wholemeal breadcrumbs
1 egg, beaten
4 spring onions, thinly sliced
280ml/½ pint pure tomato juice
30ml/2 tbsps tomato purée
Juice of half a lemon
15ml/1 tbsp honey
1 green chilli, seeded and thinly sliced
2 slices fresh pineapple, finely chopped
1 medium-sized red pepper, seeded and cut into thin strips
2 carrots, peeled and coarsely grated

1. Fry the onions gently in the olive oil until they are just transparent.

2. Using a food processor or mincer, finely chop or mince the raw turkey.

3. Put the minced turkey into a large bowl, along with the garlic, parsley, almonds, pepper, mixed spice, raisins, breadcrumbs and egg.

4. Stir in the cooked onion and the oil, mixing well to combine all ingredients thoroughly.

5. Divide the mixture into 16 and shape each piece into a small ball. Chill for 30 minutes.

Step 4 Stir the fried onions and the oil into the minced turkey mixture, mixing thoroughly to ensure that all ingredients are blended evenly.

Step 5 Divide the mixture into 16 and shape each piece into a small ball using lightly floured hands.

6. Put all the remaining ingredients into a shallow pan and bring to the boil. Cover the pan and simmer the sauce gently for 10 minutes, stirring occasionally.

7. Carefully drop the chilled meatballs into the sauce. Re-cover and simmer for a further 20 minutes, or until the meatballs are completely cooked.

Cook's Notes

Time
Preparation takes 20-25 minutes, cooking time takes about 35 minutes.

Serving Idea
Serve with brown rice or wholemeal pasta.

Preparation
If the sauce evaporates too quickly, add a little stock or water to keep it to a thin enough consistency.

Cook's Tip
The shaped meatballs can be lightly fried in a little oil before being added to the sauce, if preferred.

SERVES 4

SKATE WINGS WITH BUTTER SAUCE

*Fish of any kind is an excellent source of iodine for people who are on a low
salt diet. Skate wings are both economical and delicious,
and can make an interesting change from everyday fish dishes.*

4 wings of skate
1 very small onion, sliced
2 parsley stalks
6 black peppercorns
280ml/½ pint vegetable or fish stock
60g/4 tbsps unsalted butter
15ml/1 tbsp capers
30ml/2 tbsps white wine vinegar
15ml/1 tbsp fresh chopped parsley

1. Place the skate wings in one layer in a large deep sauté pan.

2. Add the onion slices, parsley stalks and peppercorns, then pour over the stock.

3. Bring the fish gently to the boil with the pan uncovered and allow to simmer for 10-15 minutes.

4. Carefully remove the skate wings from the pan and arrange on a serving platter.

5. Remove any skin or large pieces of bone, taking great care not the break up the fish. Keep warm.

6. Place the butter into a small pan and cook over a high heat until it begins to brown.

7. Add the capers and immediately remove the butter from the heat. Stir in the vinegar to foam the hot butter.

8. Pour the hot butter sauce over the skate wings and sprinkle with some chopped parsley. Serve immediately.

Step 5 Carefully remove any skin or large bones from the cooked fish using a small sharp pointed knife.

Step 1 Place the skate wings in a pan along with the onion slice, parsley stalks, peppercorns and stock.

Step 7 Add the vinegar to the hot butter and capers. This will cause the butter to froth.

Cook's Notes

Time
Preparation takes 10-15 minutes, cooking will take 20 minutes.

Serving Idea
Serve with fresh vegetables and new or jacket potatoes.

Preparation
When the skate is completely cooked, the meat will pull away from the bones in long strips.

Watchpoint
Take care not to burn the butter when heating it rapidly. It should only just begin to brown, before adding the capers and vinegar.

SERVES 4

CHICKEN WITH APPLE CREAM SAUCE

Fresh tasting apples and tender chicken makes this low salt recipe ideal for serving as part of a special meal.

60g/2oz unsalted butter
30ml/2 tbsps vegetable oil
8 skinned and boned chicken breasts
60ml/4 tbsps brandy
2 dessert apples, peeled, cored and coarsely chopped
1 shallot, finely chopped
2 sticks celery, finely chopped
2.5ml/½ tsp dried thyme, crumbled
90ml/6 tbsps chicken stock
2 eggs, lightly beaten
90ml/6 tbsps double cream

1. Melt half the butter and all of the oil in a large sauté pan until it is foaming.

2. Add the chicken and fry gently, turning once or twice, until each piece is well browned.

3. Pour off most of the fat from the pan, leaving just the chicken pieces and their juices to cook.

4. Pour the brandy into the pan with the chicken and heat gently. Carefully ignite the brandy with a match and shake the sauté pan until the flames subside.

5. In a small saucepan or frying pan, melt the remaining butter. Stir in the chopped apple, shallot and celery. Cook for about 5 minutes, until soft, but not brown.

6. Add the cooked apples to the chicken portions, along with the thyme and stock. Bring the chicken to the boil, cover, reduce the heat and simmer for 30 minutes.

7. Remove the chicken from the pan and arrange on a serving dish. Put the eggs and cream into a bowl and gradually whisk in some of the hot sauce from the sauté pan. Continue whisking until all the hot sauce has been added and the mixture is smooth.

8. Return the sauce to the sauté pan and heat gently over a low temperature for 2-3 minutes, stirring constantly until the sauce thickens. Pour the hot sauce over the chicken breasts and serve garnished with some watercress.

Step 4 Carefully ignite the warmed brandy, shaking the pan gently until the flames subside.

Step 7 Whisking vigorously with a balloon whisk, gradually add the hot sauce mixture to the eggs and cream, beating until smooth.

Cook's Notes

Time
Preparation takes 25-30 minutes, cooking takes 40-50 minutes.

Preparation
If preferred, the sauce can be blended using a food processor or liquidiser instead of whisking by hand.

Serving Idea
Serve with sauté potatoes and petit pois.

Watchpoint
Take great care not to allow the sauce to boil once the egg and cream is added or it will curdle.

SERVES 4

MEDITERRANEAN SHELLFISH CASSEROLE

Fresh shellfish cooked with red wine and tomatoes makes an impressive main course to serve for that special dinner party.

1 onion, peeled and finely chopped
2 cloves garlic, peeled and crushed
45ml/3 tbsps olive oil
750g/1½lbs tomatoes, skinned, seeded and chopped
30ml/2 tbsps tomato purée
570ml/1 pint dry red wine
Freshly ground black pepper
1¼ ltrs/2 pints mussels, in their shells
8 large Mediterranean prawns, in their shells
120g/4oz peeled prawns
120g/4oz white crab meat
8 small crab claws, for garnish
30ml/2 tbsps vegetable oil
1 clove garlic, crushed
1 tbsp fresh chopped parsley
8 slices stale French bread

1. In a large saucepan, fry the onion gently in the olive oil for 3 minutes, or until transparent but not browned.

2. Add the 2 cloves of garlic and chopped tomatoes to the onions, fry gently for a further 3 minutes, stirring to break up the tomatoes.

3. Stir in the tomato purée, red wine and black pepper. Bring the sauce to the boil; cover and simmer for 15 minutes.

4. Scrub the mussels to remove any small barnacles or bits of seaweed attached to the shells.

5. If any of the mussels are open, tap them gently with the handle of a knife. If they do not close up immediately, discard.

6. Drop all tightly closed mussels into the simmering tomato sauce. Cover and cook for 5 minutes.

Step 4 Trim any small barnacles or pieces of seaweed away from the mussel shells using a small, sharp knife.

Step 6 After cooking for 5 minutes in the tomato sauce, all the mussels should have opened completely. Any that do not, must be removed and discarded.

7. Add the whole prawns, peeled prawns, crab and claws to the mussels and tomatoes. Re-cover and simmer for 5 minutes.

8. Heat the vegetable oil in a frying pan and stir in the remaining garlic clove and parsley.

9. Put the slices of French bread into the hot oil and fry until brown on one side. Turn each slice over and fry until the second side is well browned.

10. Spoon the fish stew into a deep sided serving dish and arrange the garlic croutons over the top. Stir briefly before serving.

Cook's Notes

Time
Preparation takes 15-20 minutes, cooking takes about 30 minutes.

Preparation
All the mussels must have opened completely after being cooked in the tomato sauce. Any that do not, must be removed and discarded.

Serving Idea
Serve with a large mixed salad and perhaps some extra French bread to mop up the sauce.

SERVES 6

VEAL WITH SORREL AND CHEESE STUFFING

*Fresh sorrel has a delightful flavour and is often found growing
wild in the countryside or in old back gardens.
If you cannot get any, use fresh spinach instead.*

900g/2lbs rolled joint of veal
120g/4oz Philadelphia cheese with garlic and herbs
120g/4oz sorrel leaf, finely chopped
10ml/2 tsps fresh oregano or marjoram, chopped
60g/2oz finely chopped walnuts
Freshly ground black pepper
60g/2oz plain flour
2.5ml/½ tsp paprika
1 egg, beaten
120g/4oz dried breadcrumbs
45ml/3 tbsps unsalted butter, melted

Step 2 Spread the filling ingredients evenly over the inside of the joint of meat.

1. Unroll the veal joint and trim off some of the fat from the outside using a sharp knife.

2. Put the cheese, sorrel, oregano or marjoram, walnuts and black pepper into a bowl. Mix together using a round bladed knife or your hands, until the ingredients are well bound together. Spread this filling over the inside of the veal.

3. Roll the veal joint up, swiss-roll fashion, and sew the ends together with a trussing needle and thick thread.

4. Dredge the veal roll with the flour and sprinkle with the paprika. Press this coating well onto the meat using your hands.

5. Brush the floured joint liberally with beaten egg and roll it into the dried breadcrumbs, pressing gently to make sure that all surfaces are thoroughly coated.

Step 3 Sew the ends of the joint together using a trussing needle and strong thread.

6. Place the coated veal on a baking sheet, brush with melted butter and roast in a preheated oven 160°C/325°F/ Gas Mark 5, for 1 hour, or until the meat is well cooked.

7. Allow to stand for 10 minutes before slicing and serving hot, or chill and serve cold.

Cook's Notes

Time
Preparation takes 25 minutes, cooking takes 1-1½ hours.

Variation
Use a rolled joint of lamb instead of the veal.

Serving Idea
Serve with salad or vegetables and a rich brown sauce.

Freezing
This recipe will freeze well, and is ideal prepared in advance and served cold, after being thawed.

SERVES 4

POUSSINS WITH DEVILLED SAUCE

Although this recipe takes quite a while to prepare, the end result will make your effort worthwhile.

4 poussins
5ml/1 tsp each of paprika, mustard powder and ground ginger
2.5ml/½ tsp ground turmeric
1.25ml/¼ tsp ground allspice
60g/4 tbsps unsalted butter
30ml/2 tbsps chilli sauce
15ml/1 tbsp plum chutney
15ml/1 tbsp brown sauce
15ml/1 tbsp Worcestershire sauce
15ml/1 tbsp soy sauce
Dash Tabasco sauce
45ml/3 tbsps chicken stock

1. Tie the legs of each poussin together and tuck them under the wing tips.

2. Put the paprika, mustard, ginger, turmeric and allspice, into a small bowl and mix together well.

3. Rub the spice mixture evenly on all sides of the four poussins, taking great care to push some behind the wings and into the joints.

4. Refrigerate the poussins for at least 1 hour.

5. Arrange the poussins in a roasting pan. Melt the butter and brush it evenly over the birds. Roast in a preheated oven, 180°C/350°F/Gas Mark 4, for 20 minutes, brushing with the roasting juices during this time.

6. Put the chilli sauce, plum chutney, brown sauce, Worcestershire sauce, soy sauce and Tabasco and chicken stock into a small bowl and mix well.

7. Brush about half of this sauce over the poussins. Return to the oven and cook for a further 40 minutes.

8. Brush the poussins twice more with the remaining sauce mixture during this final cooking time so that the skins become brown and crisp.

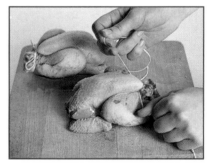

Step 1 Tie the legs of each poussin together with trussing thread and tuck them under the wing tips.

Step 3 Rub the poussins all over with the spice mixture, pressing it down into the wings and joints.

Cook's Notes

Time
Preparation takes about 25 minutes, plus 1 hour standing time. Cooking takes 60-70 minutes, depending on the size of the poussins.

Variation
Use pigeons or grouse instead of the poussins in this recipe.

Serving Idea
Serve with fresh cooked pasta and a large salad.

Freezing
This dish freezes well for up to 3 months.

SERVES 4

FIVE-SPICED PORK

*Five spice is a ready-prepared spicy powder which can easily be obtained
from delicatessens or ethnic supermarkets. It is used in this
dish with ginger and pepper to make a typical Szechwan meal.*

450g/1lb fillet pork
60ml/4 tbsps sesame oil
One 2.5cm/1-inch piece fresh ginger, peeled and
   chopped
5ml/1 tsp black peppercorns
5ml/1 tsp five spice powder
75ml/5 tbsps dry sherry
140ml/¼ pint light stock
30ml/2 tbsps honey
4 spring onions, cut into diagonal slices
60g/2oz bamboo shoots, shredded
1 large ripe mango, peeled and flesh sliced

1. Using a sharp knife, finely slice the pork fillets into thin strips.

Step 1 Using a sharp knife, shred the pork into thin strips.

2. Put the oil into a wok or large frying pan, and heat gently. Add the ginger and stir this into the oil. Fry quickly for 20-30 seconds.

Step 3 Stir-fry the meat with the oil and ginger.

Step 5 Add the onions, bamboo shoots and mango to the cooked pork, stirring continuously to cook evenly.

3. Add the sliced meat to the wok and stir-fry for 4-5 minutes, or until the meat is well cooked and tender.

4. Stir the peppercorns, five spice powder, sherry, stock and honey into the meat. Mix well and bring to the boil.

5. Add all the remaining ingredients to the wok and cook quickly, stirring all the time for a further 3 minutes.

6. Serve immediately.

Cook's Notes

Time
Preparation takes 25 minutes, cooking takes about 10 minutes.

Variation
Use chicken instead of pork in this recipe.

Serving Idea
Serve with rice or Chinese noodles.

SERVES 4

SWEET PEPPER STEAKS

*The sweet peppers in this recipe refer only to the vegetable and not
to the flavour of this dish. Peppers, mustard and capers blend
together to make a delicious spicy sauce without the need for added salt.*

4 sirloin steaks, approximately 120g/4oz each in weight
2 cloves garlic, crushed
Freshly ground black pepper
45ml/3 tbsps vegetable oil
2 shallots, finely chopped
60ml/4 tbsps capers
120g/4oz sliced mushrooms
30g/2 tbsps plain flour
280ml/½ pint dark stock
20ml/4 tsps ready-made mustard
10ml/2 tsps Worcestershire sauce
120ml/8 tbsps white wine
10ml/2 tsps lemon juice
Pinch each of dried thyme and rosemary
8 baby corn on the cobs, cut in half lengthways
1 green pepper, seeded and finely sliced
1 red pepper, seeded and finely sliced
1 yellow pepper, seeded and finely sliced
4 tomatoes, peeled, seeded and cut into thin strips

1. Lay the steaks onto a board and rub both surfaces of each with the garlic and black pepper. Refrigerate for 30 minutes.

2. Heat the oil in a large frying pan and quickly fry the steaks for 1 minute on each side. Remove the steaks from the pan and set aside.

3. Add the shallot, capers and mushrooms to the oil and meat juices in the frying pan. Cook for about 1 minute.

4. Sprinkle the flour over the vegetables and fry gently until it begins to brown. Pour over the stock and stir well, adding the mustard, Worcestershire sauce, wine, lemon juice, thyme and rosemary, as the sauce thickens.

5. Return the steaks to the sauce mixture along with the sweet corn, peppers and tomatoes. Simmer for 6-8 minutes, or until the steaks are cooked, but still pink in the centre. Serve at once.

Step 4 Sprinkle the flour over the cooked vegetables and fry gently to brown lightly.

Step 5 Stir the sweetcorn, peppers and tomatoes into the sauce, mixing well to coat evenly.

Cook's Notes

Time
Preparation takes about 30 minutes, plus 30 minutes chilling time. Cooking takes 20 minutes.

Preparation
It is important to fry the steaks initially on both sides as this helps to seal in the meats juices.

Serving Idea
Serve the steaks with rice or jacket potatoes.

SERVES 6

CHOCOLATE BRANDY MOUSSE

Dark chocolate and brandy blend together to create a delicious mousse which sets to a rich cream in the refrigerator.

180g/6oz plain chocolate
75ml water
15g/1 tbsp unsalted butter
3 eggs, separated
30ml/2 tbsps brandy
60ml/4 tbsps grated chocolate

1. Break the chocolate into small pieces and place in a large bowl with the water.

2. Stand the bowl over a saucepan which has been half filled with simmering water. Stir the chocolate and water together until they melt and combine thoroughly.

3. Remove the bowl from the saucepan and allow to cool slightly.

4. Cut the butter into small dice and add this to the melted chocolate, stirring it gently to blend it in as it melts.

5. Beat the egg yolks, one at a time, into the melted chocolate mixture, then stir in the brandy.

6. Put the egg whites into a large bowl and whisk them with an electric or hand whisk, until they are stiff, but not dry.

7. Fold these carefully into the chocolate mixture.

8. Divide the chocolate mousse between 6 serving dishes and chill overnight before serving.

9. Sprinkle with grated chocolate to serve.

Step 2 Melt the chocolate in a large bowl placed over a pan of simmering water.

Step 7 Carefully fold the whipped egg whites into the chocolate mixture using a spatula or metal spoon.

Cook's Notes

Time
Preparation takes 20 minutes, cooking takes about 10 minutes.

Variation
Add half a teaspoon of grated orange rind and 30ml/2 tbsps Cointreau in place of the brandy in this recipe.

Watchpoint
Take great care not to melt the chocolate too quickly or it will separate.

SERVES 6

HONEY AND APPLE TART

This delicious apple flan is wonderful served either hot or cold.

90g/3oz wholemeal flour
90g/3oz plain white flour
90g/3oz unsalted butter
1 egg yolk
45ml/3 tbsps cold water
280ml/½ pint unsweetened apple purée
15ml/1 tbsp honey
2 egg yolks
30ml/2 tbsps ground almonds
3 large eating apples, quartered, cored and thinly sliced
Little pale soft brown sugar
45ml/3 tbsps clear honey, warmed to glaze

soft dough and adding a little extra water if necessary.

4. Roll the dough on a lightly floured surface and line a 22.5 cm/9-inch loose-bottom, fluted flan ring. Pinch up the edges well and prick the base to prevent it from rising during cooking.

5. Mix the apple purée with the honey, egg yolks and ground almonds, stirring well to blend thoroughly.

6. Spread this apple mixture evenly over the base of the pastry case.

7. Arrange the apple slices, overlapping slightly, in circles on the top of the apple and almond filling.

Step 4 Pinch the edges of the flan up, and prick the base with a fork.

Step 7 Arrange the apple slices, overlapping each slice slightly in circles, on the top of the apple and almond filling.

1. Put the flours into a large bowl.

2. Cut the butter into small pieces and rub these into the flour until the mixture resembles fine breadcrumbs.

3. Beat the egg yolk and 30ml/2 tbsps of the water together. Stir this into the dry ingredients, mixing to a firm

8. Sprinkle the top of the flan lightly with a little soft brown sugar, and bake in a preheated oven 190°C/375°F/Gas Mark 5 for 35-40 minutes, or until the apples are just beginning to go golden brown.

9. As soon as the flan is removed from the oven, carefully brush the top with the warmed honey glaze.

Cook's Notes

 Time
Preparation takes 45 minutes, cooking takes about 40 minutes.

 Serving Idea
Serve with fresh whipped cream.

 Watchpoint
If the apples begin to brown before the end of cooking time, cover the tart with aluminium foil to prevent any further colouring.

SERVES 6-8
PRUNE, APRICOT AND NUT FLAN

This sumptuous sweet tart has a nutty shortcake pastry for its base.

120g/4oz dried apricots
120g/4oz dried prunes
280ml/½ pint red wine, or dry cider
120g/4oz unsalted butter
60g/2oz soft brown sugar
120g/4oz plain flour
60g/2oz ground hazelnuts
45ml/3 tbsps finely chopped walnuts
30ml/2 tbsps clear honey, warmed

Step 4 Work the chopped walnuts into the pastry as you knead it.

Step 3 Gradually fold the ground hazelnuts and flour into the creamed butter and sugar until it forms a soft dough.

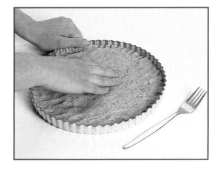

Step 5 Press the shortcake pastry evenly over the base of a loose-bottomed flan tin.

1. Put the apricots and prunes into a large bowl. Warm the wine or cider, and pour it over the dried fruit. Leave to stand for 4 hours minimum.

2. Put the butter and sugar into a large bowl and cream it together until it becomes light and fluffy.

3. Gradually stir in the flour and ground hazelnuts.

4. Knead the dough lightly until it is smooth, working in the chopped walnuts as you go.

5. Press the shortcake dough evenly over the base of a 22.5cm/9-inch fluted loose-bottomed flan tin. Prick the surface of the dough with a fork and bake in a preheated oven, 190°C/375°F/Gas Mark 5, for 15 minutes.

6. Remove the prunes and apricots from the soaking liquid and drain them thoroughly on absorbent paper.

7. Remove the shortcake from the oven and arrange the fruit over the hot shortcake.

8. Cover the tart with aluminium foil and return to the oven for a further 10 minutes.

9. Remove the shortcake carefully from its tin and arrange on a serving plate.

10. While the shortcake is still hot, brush the fruit with the warmed honey to glaze.

Cook's Notes

 Time
Preparation takes 30 minutes, plus soaking time. Cooking takes 25 minutes.

 Watchpoint
If the shortcake mixture is too soft to handle, chill it in a refrigerator for 30 minutes.

 Freezing
This dessert freezes well for up to 2 months, but should be glazed just before serving.

SERVES 4

SPICED CRÈME BRÛLÉE

Delight your guests with this unusual variation of a classic dish

280ml/½ pint milk
1 stick cinnamon
10ml/2 tbsps whole coriander seeds
1 vanilla pod
4 egg yolks
25ml/1½ tbsps cornflour
90g/3oz caster sugar
280ml/½ pint double cream
60ml/4 tbsps demerara or light soft brown sugar

1. Put the milk into a heavy-based saucepan and add the cinnamon, coriander and vanilla pod. Heat gently until the mixture begins to boil. Remove from the heat and cool completely.

2. In a bowl, whisk the egg yolks, cornflour and the sugar together to form a soft, light mousse.

3. Strain the milk through a sieve to remove the spices. Put the strained milk into a saucepan along with the cream, and heat until just below boiling point.

4. Beat the hot milk and cream into the egg yolk mixture, pouring gradually and mixing constantly to ensure a smooth batter.

5. Rinse out the saucepan and return the custard to it. Cook over a very gentle heat until almost boiling, stirring all the time with a wooden spoon until the mixture is thick enough to coat the back of it.

6. Divide the custard equally between 4 heat resistant serving dishes. Chill until set.

7. Stand the individual custards into a roasting pan and surround them with ice. Preheat a grill to its highest temperature.

8. Sprinkle 15ml/1 tbsp of the brown sugar evenly over the top of each custard and then put under the grill. Turn the custards frequently and move the pan around until the sugar melts and caramelises. Discard the ice and return the custards to the refrigerator. Chill until the sugar layer is hard and crisp.

Step 2 Whisk the egg yolks, cornflour and sugar together until they are light and creamy. When lifted, this mixture should leave a trail on its surface.

Step 5 Cook the custard very gently until it is thick enough to coat the back of a wooden spoon.

Step 7 Stand the dishes of custard in a roasting pan and surround them with broken ice to prevent the custards from heating when grilled.

COOK'S NOTES

Time
Preparation takes 15 minutes, cooking takes 30 minutes.

Serving Idea
Serve with biscuits or fresh fruit.

Watchpoint
Do not boil either the milk and cream mixture or the egg yolk mixture, as this will result in curdling and the custard will not be smooth.

SERVES 4

CINNAMON CŒUR À LA CRÈME WITH RASPBERRY SAUCE

Delicious cinnamon creams are complemented delightfully by the sharp raspberry sauce.

225g/8oz cream cheese
400ml/12 fl oz whipping cream
90g/3oz icing sugar, sifted
10ml/2 tsps ground cinnamon
225g/8oz fresh raspberries
30g/1oz icing sugar

1. Put the cream cheese into a large bowl along with 60ml/4 tbsps of the cream. Whisk with an electric mixer until the mixture is light and fluffy.

2. Mix in the 3oz of icing sugar and the cinnamon, stirring well until all ingredients are well blended.

3. Whip the remaining cream in another bowl until it forms soft peaks.

4. Fold the cream into the cheese mixture with a metal spoon.

5. Line four individual Cœur à la Crème moulds with dampened muslin or clean damp J-cloths, extending the material beyond the edges of the moulds.

6. Spoon the cheese mixture into the mould and spread out evenly, pressing down well to remove any air bubbles.

7. Fold the overlapping edges of the muslin or J-cloth over the top of the mixture, and refrigerate the moulds on a rack placed over a tray, for at least 8 hours.

8. Purée the raspberries in a liquidiser or food processor, and press through a nylon sieve to remove all the pips.

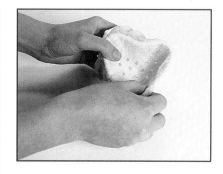

Step 5 Line four individual Cœur à la Crème moulds with dampened muslin or clean, damp J-cloths, extending the material beyond the edges of the moulds.

Step 7 Stand the Cœur à la Crème moulds on a rack over a tray to collect the drips when refrigerated.

9. Blend the 1oz of icing sugar into the fruit purée to sweeten.

10. Carefully remove the cheesecloth from the cream cheese hearts, and place each one on a serving dish.

11. Spoon a little of the sauce over each heart and serve the remainder separately.

Cook's Notes

Time
Preparation takes 15 minutes, plus overnight refrigerating.

Preparation
It is important to use proper Cœur à la Crème moulds as these have small holes in the base which allow any excess liquid to drain off during the chilling time.

Serving Idea
Serve these cream cheese desserts with a little extra whipped cream and candied rose petals.

MAKES 10-12 TEACAKES
SAFFRON TEACAKES

The use of sweet spices in baking will reduce the necessity to add salt to recipes.

140ml/¼ pint milk
Good pinch saffron
225g/8oz self-raising flour
120g/4oz unsalted butter
120g/4oz currants
2.5ml/½ tsp allspice
30g/1oz candied peel
60g/2oz caster sugar
1 egg, beaten

1. Heat 60ml/4 tbsps of the milk in a small saucepan and add the saffron. Allow to stand for 10-15 minutes to infuse.

2. Sift the flour into a large bowl and cut the butter into this with a knife, until it is reduced to very small pieces.

3. Stir the currants, allspice, peel and sugar into the flour and butter mixture.

4. Make a well in the centre of the flour and stir in the saffron milk and the remainder of the milk. Mix well to form a soft dough

5. Turn the dough onto a lightly floured board, and knead until smooth.

6. Roll the dough into a circle approximately 1.25cm/½ -inch thick. Cut into 10-12 rounds with a 7.5cm/3-inch pastry cutter.

7. Arrange the individual rounds on a lightly greased baking sheet, and brush the top with a little beaten egg.

8. Bake the cakes in a preheated oven, 180°C/350°F/ Gas Mark 4, for 20-30 minutes, until they are well risen and golden brown.

Step 1 Allow the saffron to infuse in the hot milk until it is golden.

Step 2 Using a round-bladed knife, cut the butter into the flour until it is finely chopped.

Step 4 Mix the milk into the flour from the centre of the bowl, drawing the flour into the liquid gradually.

Cook's Notes

Time
Preparation takes 15 minutes, cooking will take 20-30 minutes.

Cook's Tip
Do not be tempted to use too much saffron; a little will go a very long way.

Freezing
These teacakes freeze very well for up to 1 month.

MAKES ONE 17.5cm/7-inch SQUARE CAKE

GINGERBREAD

Dark treacle and fresh ginger combine to make this favourite family cake.

120g/4oz unsalted butter
120ml/4 fl oz black treacle
225g/8oz light soft brown sugar
120ml/4 fl oz hot water
300g/10oz plain flour
10ml/2 tsps baking powder
10ml/2 tsps fresh ginger, peeled and grated
5ml/1 tsp grated nutmeg
1 egg, beaten

Step 4 Gradually beat in the treacle, using a wooden spoon and drawing the flour from the outside into the centre.

Step 1 Melt the butter, treacle and sugar together in a large saucepan.

Step 6 The cake is done when a skewer inserted into the centre comes out clean.

1. Put the butter into a large saucepan, along with the treacle and sugar. Heat gently, stirring all the time, until the sugar and butter have melted together.

2. Pour in the hot water, mix well and set aside.

3. Sift the flour with the baking powder into a large bowl. Make a well in the centre, and add the ginger, nutmeg and beaten egg.

4. Gradually beat in the treacle, using a wooden spoon and drawing the flour from the outside into the centre gradually.

5. Line the base of the cake tin with silicone or lightly greased greaseproof paper.

6. Pour the gingerbread mixture into the cake tin, and bake in a preheated oven 160°C/325°F/Gas Mark 3, for 1-1½ hours, testing during this time with a skewer; which should come out clean when the cake is cooked.

7. Allow the cake to cool in the tin, before turning out onto a wire rack.

Cook's Notes

 Time
Preparation takes about 15 minutes, cooking takes 1-1½ hours.

 Variation
Add 60g/2oz chopped mixed fruit to the gingerbread mixture along with the spices.

 Serving Idea
Serve as a dessert with a lemon sauce.

 Freezing
This cake freezes well for up to 1 month.

MAKES ONE 20cm/8-inch ROUND CAKE

ALMOND LAYER GATEAU

Definitely not for the diet conscious, but delicious for those wishing to sin. This wonderful creamy gateau is ideal for serving with tea, or even as a dessert.

60g/2oz dried white breadcrumbs
120ml/4 fl oz milk
30ml/2 tbsps rum
90g/3oz unsalted butter or margarine
90g/3oz caster sugar
6 eggs, separated
90g/3oz ground roasted almonds
570ml/1 pint double cream
30g/2 tbsps icing sugar
60g/2oz roasted almonds, finely chopped
Whole blanched almonds, lightly toasted for decoration

1. Put the breadcrumbs into a large bowl and pour over the milk and 15ml/1 tbsp of the rum. Allow to stand for 15 minutes or until the liquid has been completely absorbed.

2. Put the butter in a large bowl and beat until soft. Gradually add the sugar and continue mixing until it is light and fluffy.

3. Beat the egg yolks, one at a time, into the butter mixture. Stir well to prevent it curdling.

4. Add the soaked breadcrumbs to the egg and butter mixture, folding them well to blend evenly.

5. Whisk the egg whites until they are stiff, but not dry.

Fold these into the egg and butter mixture, along with the ground almonds.

6. Lightly grease three 20cm/8-inch round cake tins, and dust each one lightly with a little flour. Line the base of each tin with silicone paper or lightly greased greaseproof paper.

7. Divide the cake mixture equally between the three tins. Bake in a preheated oven 180°C/350°F/Gas Mark 4, for 30-35 minutes, until well risen and golden brown.

8. Allow the cakes to cool briefly in the tins before gently loosening the sides and turning onto a wire rack to cool completely.

9. Whip the cream until it is stiff, then beat in the icing sugar and remaining rum.

10. Reserve one third of the cream in a separate bowl, and fold the finely chopped almonds into the remaining two-thirds.

11. Sandwich the cake layers together with the almond cream, then spread the plain cream onto the top, reserving some for piping.

12. Fit a piping bag with a small rosette nozzle and pipe rosettes of cream onto the top of the cake. Decorate with the toasted whole almonds and serve.

Step 3 Beat the egg yolks, one at a time, into the butter and sugar mixture, mixing well to prevent curdling.

Step 11 Sandwich the layers of the cake together with the almond cream, pressing them down gently so that the cream shows around the edge.

Cook's Notes

Time
Preparation takes 40 minutes, cooking takes 35 minutes.

Cook's Tip
Refrigerate the cream for at least 2 hours before whipping, to obtain better results.

Freezing
The almond cakes can be frozen for up to 1 month, but should be filled and decorated just before serving or they will become too soggy.

Index

COMPILED BY PATRICIA PAYNE
EDITED BY JILLIAN STEWART
PHOTOGRAPHY BY PETER BARRY
RECIPES STYLED BY HELEN BURDETT
DESIGNED BY SALLY STRUGNELL
COVER DESIGN BY MARILYN O'NEONS